# Stepping Stones

## By

## Kathleen Driver

# GRATITUDE

*All glory, honor and praise to God for all that He created me to be.*

*To my mother (Hazel) and father (Samuel),*
*who loved me unconditionally,*
*I honor you and love you and always hold you in my heart.*
*I am who I am because of who you were.*

*Many thanks to my family who believe in me even when I don't always believe in myself: Norma, Fred, Jonathan, Herbert, Randolph, Brian and Dennis.*

*Angela, thank you for encouraging me to write.*

# INTRODUCTION

*"The difference between a stepping stone and a
stumbling block is how you pick up your feet."*
- Unknown

What happens to us when we get a big title or
a huge responsibility?

Some of us feel like we are defined by the title
and are always in that role, sometimes forgetting to
acknowledge, nurture and take care of the woman
inside.

Don't you want to just let it all go occasionally
and just be real without speaking from the labels that
you and others have placed upon you?  Don't you
want to release the façade, if only just for a moment?

Whatever we go through in life, we are not the
only ones.  We are not the first, nor the last to have
the experience.  That's the good news (and perhaps
the bad news).  We are emotional by nature, and we
can appreciate knowing that someone else went
through what we are going through.  It gives us
comfort to know that someone else knows what we
are going through, and they made it through.
'Through' being the operative word.  It's not to say
that we have ill-wishes towards each other, it's just a
semblance of comfort and a bonding agent knowing
that we are not alone in our experiences.

We've all heard the saying, "You think you've
got it bad until you hear someone else's story."  Once
we start to share our stories, we find that our situa-

tion may not be as bad as it originally seemed after the sister you are sharing with (whatever ethnicity) starts to open up to share her own experience. I've found that although transparency is not easy, it can be so valuable as long as trust is the foundation. The best part of sharing and being transparent is the mutual motivation, help and understanding.

Our internal chatter can be discouraging and we often 'think' ourselves out of acting on inspirations that could allow us to progress, to follow our passion or to be and do what we really want. It's natural and smart to think through ideas, but often, the internal dialogue of doubt takes over, and we submit to it and decisively stay in our comfort zones. The comfort zone may not be the place we want to be, but it's the place that we know. No matter how bad it might be, it still feels safe because it's familiar to us. Our dreams usually take us to places unknown.

I struggled with following my passion, which is writing and not giving myself permission to be a writer. I was afraid of stepping outside of my self-constructed box. I allowed fear to prevent me from sharing a novel that I had published which received rave reviews from those who had read it. I was having a conversation with a trusted, close friend about why it is so hard to give ourselves approval to do the things in life that we really want to do and need to do when she reminded me of many times prior that I had actually given myself permission to make a difficult decision or to move outside of my comfort zone. In retrospect, I recalled positive results and ultimately valuable growth experiences as well, after being reminded by my friend.  I also re-called that, with each experience, I was unable to move forward until I reconciled my internal dialogue. It was out of that conversation that the concept for this book was born.  Thank you, Angela.

Although the story that you are about to read is fictional, based on fictional characters, their experiences and conversations are familiar, honest and sincere.

# Chapter 1

## PERMISSION TO DREAM

*"There is only one thing that makes a dream impossible to achieve: the fear of failure."*
— Paulo Coelho, The Alchemist

*I've made it to 'hump day,'* Kitt thought as she admired herself in the full-length mirror she had personally installed in her modest condominium.  She was dressed in one of her favorite red, power suits as she liked to think of it.  She had an important meeting today, and she was told that red was a good color for her. *The things we have to do as women, but you are working it, girl!*

Kitt arrived to work on time, despite the horrendous rush hour traffic getting into Downtown, Anytown.  Although she had been doing this drive for ten years, it didn't get any easier.  She said, "Good Morning" to her co-workers as she passed them on her way to her tiny cubicle.  The workspace always seemed to bring her mood down.  She thought that anyone with as much responsibility as she, deserved to work in privacy.  Kitt was a social media marketing designer for a major corporation, and it was difficult, at best, to think through and bring designs to life for her customers with the noise and chatter around her.

*This place sucks!*
*I can't believe that they won't give me my own office!*
*Having everyone work in a bullpen like this obviously makes sense to someone, but not to me!*
*How do they expect us to work with all of this noise going on around us all of the time?*
*I wonder what they would do if I resign!*
*I can surely make more money someplace else.*
*They don't appreciate all that I do for them.*
*If I had my own business, I would respect my employees and let them all have their own office.*
*How would I ever be able to have my own business?*

Kitt decided to stop the random internal chatter exploding in her thoughts so that she could focus on her work. She managed to tune out some of the noises all around her and tune into her internal intelligence, using both sides of her brain to continue work on her current project. She used the right side of her brain for creativity and the left side for logic.

She was in her groove when she heard someone approach her. That was the worst part of this office design. Her back was to the opening of her cubicle, and it made her so uncomfortable, feeling the intrusion of having someone walk in unknowingly from behind.

It was one of the consultants that her boss had hired to help with some of the higher visibility projects.

"Hey, good morning, Kitt," he said flashing a full set of veneers. *He must be making good money; nice dental work.*

"Good morning, John." Kitt waited for him to speak next, not knowing why he was standing in her cubicle.

"I need some help with a design that I'm working on, and I was told that you are the best, and you could help me. I heard that you are the 'go-to person' to work through the difficult challenges."

*Really? So, if I'm helping you, why is my boss paying YOU the big bucks and I'm living paycheck to paycheck and working in this tiny-ass cubicle while you are working in an office with a door?!*

"Sure, I'm happy to help you. Pull up a chair and let's take a look at it."

"Umm. Can you come to my office? It's much quieter there."

*Yeah, I'll come to your damn office. It should be my office!*

Kitt and John worked together on his problem until mid-afternoon past her normal lunch time, but she decided to take a much-needed break. So much for her own project, but she had helped John work through his design issue. She needed some fresh air before her late-afternoon meeting and was glad she decided to step out of the office if only for a few minutes.  She ran into her best friend, April, who was returning from her lunch break.  She obviously had spent most of her lunch break shopping; she had a shopping bag in each hand and one on her wrist.  April was a lawyer with a prestigious law firm in Downtown, Anytown.

"Hey, girl!" April called to Kitt.  "Taking a late lunch?"

"Yep.  I would have been out sooner, but I was helping one of our highly paid consultants with a problem he was having," Kitt said sarcastically.

Sensing that Kitt needed to talk, April fell into step with her.  As soon as they reached a restaurant with outside seating, April invited her to grab a table so that they could continue their conversation. Once they were seated, with two of April's bags securely placed in one of the chairs and the other under the table, April pressed, "Tell me what's up.  I can tell that you are not happy right now."

Kitt took a deep breath, exhaled and spoke honestly, "I'm just really tired of giving more than one hundred percent of myself, only to work in a tiny cubicle, never really being acknowledged by my boss to now helping a highly paid consultant that was brought in to help US.  I had to stop working on my own project this morning to help him.  Maybe it's just me, but something is not right with that picture." Kitt was relieved to vent and share her frustrations with April.  They had always been a good sounding board for each other.

April was always straight and to the point; it must be the lawyer in her. "I hear you, sister.  But, I don't understand why you don't take your talent someplace else where you will be appreciated and paid for your talent and skill." *Because I'm in this comfortable little box*, Kitt heard in her thoughts.

"I'm not sure why I don't just move on.  Maybe I could start my own business." *Oh my gosh! Did I really say that?  April will think I'm crazy!  She would never support my dream...*

*In college, I dreamed of being a successful business owner of a night club - of all things.  I visualized the music playing, people dancing, sitting at the bar talking and laughing and just having a good time.  I even saw myself all dressed up, greeting and mingling with my loyal customers.  After seeing the effects of alcohol to those who over indulge, that dream fizzled.  I did not want to potentially be responsible for serving alcohol to someone who suffered from alcoholism or someone not responsible enough to not drive after drinking.*

*I used to have really big dreams.  I actually set aside time every night before going to sleep and every morning before getting out of bed to spend time in my dreams.  I became what I was dreaming about.  It was the best feeling!*

*Then I entered the real world, the corporate world that would become my comfort zone no matter how bad I thought it was.  There was no more time for dreaming.*

"Now that is a good idea!  Why don't you start your own business?  I can help you with the legal stuff, and I know a good accountant that can help you with the financial stuff," April said waiting for a response from Kitt.

*Huh?!  Where did that come from?  Is she crazy?  Where would I get customers?*

"Seriously, girl?  I don't know… how would I get customers?" *Answer that one, Ms. Smarty-Pants.*

"You put together a marketing plan and ask for referrals from some of the customers you've worked for.  You don't want to take those customers from your current employer, but they might be willing to refer work to you from other companies.  You also do a lot of free work for your church.  Let them know that you are starting your own business and watch them support you and refer customers to you!  And you start networking with professional organiza-tions."

*It all sounds good.  But, what will other people think?  Up to this point, I've always worked at the same place.  Will they take me seriously as a business owner?*

"You make it all sound so easy and exciting.  But, should I walk away from a guaranteed salary, although so low I'm barely making ends meet, to start a business?  Isn't it risky?"

"Yes, there is always a risk.  But, make sure that you have at least three months of expenses in the bank.  Maybe you could ask for "Angel" investors among your friends and family.   There are also local resources that assist small businesses that you could tap into.  You know what?  You won't know how it turns out unless you try," April said with an assured smile.  Kitt remembered a saying that she had heard almost her entire life, *nothing beats a failure but a try.*

Bravely verbalizing the doubts ringing in her head, Kitt shared what she was thinking with April.  "You are right, but will anyone take me seriously as a business owner?  How can I go from working for someone else to working for myself?  What will people think?"

"Ah!  So, is that what is really holding you back?  What others think?  Do you need other people to validate who you are and your capabilities?  Here is what you do:  you go from working for someone else to coming up with a plan and creating an effective team to start your business."

For effect, April leaned in towards Kitt to be closer to her before she said, "You give yourself permission to try."

# Chapter 2

## PERMISSION TO STEP OUT ON FAITH
*"Truly I tell you, if you have faith as small as a mustard seed... nothing will be impossible for you."*
- Jesus, The Holy Bible

Within a few months and after reconciling her internal dialogue, Kitt took the leap of faith into the business world as her own boss.  She took April's advice and made sure that she built her savings to sustain her for three months, just in case...

Kitt also built a support team of professionals willing to assist her with accounting and operational setup.  As promised, April came through with the legal support.  Kitt set up a home office, which was relatively easy, so she focused some of her time and energy setting up her web presence with a website and intelligent social media strategies.  Her website and social media pages had to be the best since that was a significant portion of her service offerings to potential customers.

Kitt used her professional and personal network to land her first contract for services before tendering her resignation.  It was a small contract, but she knew that *everyone has to start somewhere.* Plus, she was able to charge double what she was making as someone else's employee.  She was excited and officially bitten by the entrepreneurial bug.  She was working on the marketing project for her first customer when she received the pivotal phone call.

"Good Afternoon, this is Kitt.  How may I help you?"  She was even excited that the business telephone line that she had installed in her home was actually ringing.

"Hi, Kitt.  This is Sharon Smith."  *Huh?  Why is the contract manager from my old job calling me?*

"Hi, Sharon," Kitt responded not concealing her surprise very well.  "How are you?"  *I don't know what else to say.*

"I would be better if you hadn't left," Sharon said with honesty.  She wanted to cut to the chase with Kitt because she knew that Kitt would appreciate it.  "Some of our best customers that you served are not happy that we let you leave."

"Wait!  I did not take any customers when I left!  I know that is against the company policy," Kitt shouted out.

"No, that's not what I'm saying.  We all know that you honored your obligation to us when you left.  We would like to contract with you for your services."  Again, cutting to the chase, "When would you be able to start?"

Taken aback, Kitt responded first by saying, "Thank you."  In her mind, that was the first rule of exemplary customer service.  Show your appreciation, because without customers, there is no business.  "Is the company willing to pay my rate?"

*Probably not.* Kitt expected a negotiation war and had already decided how much she would be willing to give in order to land this business.

"Absolutely. I've already been to your website to get an idea of your rates to return to us as a consultant. We know your work, and we are willing to enter into a six-month contract with you which will keep your former customers happy and so that you can train someone else. Just between us, our Vice-President told me to do whatever is needed to make this happen. I just need you to say 'yes' and tell me when you can start. How about Monday? That will give us time to get through the contractual process."

*That's only three business days! They must really want this to happen. A six-month contract! Wow! Okay, okay, get a grip, girl!*

Kitt stopped the cart wheels that she was doing in her head and said as calmly and profession-ally as possible, "Sure. I can make that work. Just e-mail the contract and I will ask my attorney to review it and return it as soon as possible." *I have an attorney who reviews my legal documents! You go, girl!*

"I just pressed 'send'; the contract should be in your Inbox in a few seconds. Thanks a lot, Kitt. You are saving us, and we look forward to seeing you on Monday," Sharon said before disconnecting the call.

Kitt couldn't wait to hear a dial tone so that she could call April. She recited the entire conversation to her best friend who listed patiently and smiled at her friend's excitement.

"Can you believe it?!  They are willing to pay me double what I was making as an employee to return as a consultant and do the same job that I was doing before?  I can't believe it!"

April always had confidence in Kitt, but sensed that although Kitt had confidence in herself, she was not comfortable showing it. "Believe it, girl!  See what self-approval can do?" April said with a sense of satisfaction of being right.

# Chapter 3

## PERMISSION TO SUCCEED

*"I feel that luck is preparation meeting opportunity."*
- Oprah Winfrey


Kitt was "making it happen" in the business world and settled very contentedly into a new comfort zone. She was glad that she had allowed herself to follow her dream. A six-month contract turned into a twelve-month contract with her former employer. She kept their customers satisfied and was able to train and transition another professional to take over once the contract term concluded. That time also afforded Kitt the opportunity to take on some smaller projects which she worked simul-taneously. She put in a lot of hours, but this work was her current passion and right now, it was sweet!

Just as she was ending her service with her former employer, a large contract with a larger firm presented itself. Kitt thought it was a good business move to throw her hat in the ring and bid on the contract. Although she was just a one-woman show, she had the unique expertise that was being solicited. She felt that she had nothing to lose by bidding for the work. At worst, she would not get it, but at best she would win a small part of it.

At the Bidder's Conference, Kitt was approached by the Vice-President of a male dominated company that was also bidding. Somehow, he had heard about her and her expertise and approached her to discuss the opportunity to partner with his company, AnyCompany. He told Kitt that partnering with his company would assure her a portion of the contract.

He acknowledged to Kitt that he knew that she had the expertise, but he felt that they brought the "big guns" because they had a bigger name and a bigger company and because of that, they would win the contract. The catch was that Kitt would have to withdraw her bid and instead allow the company to submit her as a resource of theirs.

Initially, Kitt was offended by his approach, but after re-thinking it, she pushed her ego aside because she saw the benefit of working with a larger company; even if it did mean that it would not be apparent that she was a subcontractor to them. She agreed to the relationship as long as they paid her the rate that she demanded. The Vice-President agreed, and they shook hands to seal the deal.

They were awarded a three-month contract as a trial to a potentially longer term agreement. Kitt was holding up her end of the agreement and provided stellar service to their customer, although she suspected that all was not well between the customer and the company that she had affiliated with. The relationship between them had soured somehow. On the last day of the contract, the Vice-President of AnyCompany decided it was not in their interest to extend services with the customer.  Since it was the last day of the contract, they were leaving the customer in a bind with no support.  It all went down in a Friday afternoon meeting which Kitt was not invited to, but heard afterwards that the stinky you-know-what had hit the fan.

Not believing that the company was not going to sign a contract extension, the customer grasped for dear life to try to formulate a viable plan so they would not suffer the consequences on Monday morning.  No one was prepared for what it would mean to not have service until that fateful meeting and it became clear that the company was not interested nor did they have any intentions of serving the customer any further.  The customer asked if they could at least contract for Kitt's services to tide them over until they could come up with another, more long-term plan.  Much to everyone's surprise, the Vice-President of AnyCompany's response was, "She is an independent consultant.  She doesn't work for us.  If you want her, ask her."

Kitt was on her way out of the back entrance, looking forward to her weekend, when she heard the customer's Procurement Officer running down the hallway calling her name.  When he caught up with her, out of breath, he recanted the conversation that had taken place in the meeting.  Kitt was totally shocked at the Vice-President's response.  She believed that he was so cavalier and reckless with this statement because he truly thought that she couldn't deliver.  She recalled the conversation they'd had at the bidder's conference when he informed her that she needed them in order to be included in the project.  The Procurement Officer asked Kitt if she was willing to continue service through a direct contractual agreement with them.  Seeing it as a seamless transition and formality of paperwork, Kitt agreed, trying to hide her excitement.

She was not prepared to be asked to start on the following Monday morning.  However, that was not the request that started the panic in her mind and that she hoped was not showing on her face when the Procurement Manager asked, "We need at least four other consultants to also start on Monday.  If you can do that, the contract is yours for the next six months."

"No problem," Kitt responded, swallowing hard.  *Where the hell am I going to get four qualified resources to start on Monday?!*  "We will see you on Monday.  Have a nice weekend."

Kitt jumped in her car, thoughts already racing.  Various colleagues that she had worked with previously raced through her mind as she frantically drove home, ditching the plans that she had made for a fun weekend.  *This is business, and I have to deliver!*  Kitt kept thinking and praying.  Praying and thinking.  She made the first phone call while still driving, to a highly qualified marketing specialist, Beth, who she had recently heard might be available. Thank God that she was, and she could start on Monday!

Kitt and Beth started to brainstorm others who they had worked with in the past that might be available. They divided a list of about twelve potential candidates, some in other states that might be able help, at least temporarily to get the consulting engagement started. Some phone calls resulted in immediate affirmative responses of either needing a job or being available to help them get started. Other calls led to references of other possible marketing specialists that might be interested and available.

Monday morning seemed to roll around much faster than normal, but Kitt walked into the Procurement Officer's office with five resumes, including her own, of professionals who would be starting within the hour to support his organization.

Word travels fast. It wasn't long before the Vice-President of AnyCompany called Kitt on her cell phone Monday afternoon to give her a piece of his mind. His ego was terribly bruised. "I just don't understand why you stabbed me in the back! I should have known better. You would not have this customer without me. Why did you go around us to get this business? I should never have trusted you!"

When Kitt could finally get a word in, she said, "It was my understanding that you gave them permission to contract with me directly."

He laughed.  "Maybe I did, but I didn't think that you would go for it!"  Before this incident, he had always treated Kitt like his equal and talked to her with respect. "You have no idea what you are doing. You are not capable of handling this customer by yourself.  You need us, and you better fix this!  Get us back in there, or else!"

*You must have lost your mind!* "Really? 'Or else,' what?  It was your decision to end the contract, not mine or the customer.  They practically begged you to stay.  You thought you were throwing me under the bus when you gave them permission to contract with me directly.  You didn't think that I would be able to deliver.  Now your ego is bruised.  I would recommend that you get over it!  Right now, I have to go.  MY customer is waiting for me to start a meeting for them," Kitt said and disconnected the call with a definitive click of the 'end call' button.

*He has a nerve!  Argggggg!* Kitt heard the screaming in her head.  She took a deep breath before picking up her cell phone to call April.  She repeated the conversation she had with the Vice-President to April. "I am so pissed off at him.  This is just a case of someone trying to flex their profes-sional muscle.  I just want to make sure that I have not violated the contractual agreement that we had."

Already looking at the contract, April responded, "No, you are not in violation.  You are in good shape.  He verbally and publically granted permission for the customer to engage your services.

That's my professional opinion.  My personal opinion is, you go girl!  How did you ever get everyone lined up so quickly?  You are totally in business now!  You have just grown your business almost overnight.  I am so proud of you!"  After she had offered her personal kudos to Kitt, April went back into lawyer mode.  "Now send me the names and addresses of your employees so that we can finalize their employment contracts.  We want to make sure that everything is in order."

> *OMG!*
> *What have I done?*
> *I have employees now!*
> *How did this happen?*
> *What was I thinking?*
> *Did I jump in too fast?*
> *Am I in over my head?*
> *Is the VP of AnyCompany right about me not being able to do this?*

"Kitt?  Are you still there?" April asked.

"I'm here, but April - what have I done?  Suppose Mister Vice-President is right that I don't know what I'm doing and I really can't handle this alone?"

"Listen to me.  Don't sell yourself short.  Others may.  Others will.  But, don't buy into it.  Stay focused on yourself and your business.  You worked with AnyCompany to do a good job for your customer and it was recognized and appreciated.  It was their decision to walk away.  They did a one-eighty when they heard that you were going to continue to provide service.  The reaction from the V.P. was part ego and part business knowing that you now have the revenue that he could have had.  The bottom line is that you haven't done anything wrong.  You were presented with an opportunity that allows you to grow your business.  Sure, there is now some bad-will between you and AnyCompany, but you didn't cause it and your customer sees them for who they really are.  Regretfully, you have just experienced the ugly side of business."

"I hear you.  But, it shouldn't be this difficult."

"Suck it up and enjoy your success," April said with a smile. She was glad that she could be real with her friend and knowing that Kitt had not yet realized what she had accomplished, nor what a savvy business woman she was becoming.

# Chapter 4

## PERMISSION TO APPRECIATE

*"And what do friends do? They share, they trust, they laugh, they have common interests. And if you're not sharing, trusting, laughing and having common interests, then you don't have a solid, underlying friendship."*
- Dr. Phillip McGraw

Kitt walked into the Ritz Carlton Tea Room and was immediately greeted by the Hostess in Charge, Henri.  Henri recognized Kitt immediately.  She was often on duty when Kitt held meetings in the Tea Room with her customers and potential customers.  She admired how Kitt carried herself and conducted her business.  She thought that Kitt was a true example of success coupled with sophistication.

"Good Afternoon, Ms. Kitt.  We have your table ready for you. You are expecting six guests for High Tea, correct?"

*She remembers my name!  Well, alright!*  Kitt had an ego moment.  "Yes, Henri," Kitt said reading the gold name badge on Henri's starched, white ruffled blouse.  Henri showed Kitt to her table that was elegantly set with fine china tea cups, saucers, tea pots and small plates, accessorized with gold flatware.  Kitt was pleased with the setup and took her seat in the oversized antique red and gold chair at the head of the table.  Waiting until she was comfortably seated, Henri offered, "Can I bring you a glass of champagne while you wait for your guests to arrive?"

"Absolutely!  That will be nice," Kitt graciously accepted.  *I'm loving this!  High Tea is one of my favorite things.  I'm glad to be able to share this with my friends.*

Henri returned with Kitt's champagne and April.  Kitt knew that April would be the first to arrive. She was never late, and she loved High Tea as much as Kitt.  She had been the one to introduce it to Kitt. Kitt stood to hug her friend.  "Smooches, lady!  You look wonderful," Kitt said as she kissed April on the cheek.  April was dressed impeccably as always.

"Thank you.  You are looking marvelous yourself!  Look at you!  Everything must be going well for you," she said with a smile.

"Pretty good," Kitt replied trying to hide her happiness and excitement about her life.

"Wow, this table setting is fabulous.  Who else are you expecting?"

"The most important guest is already here," Kitt joked with her friend, feeding her ego.  They laughed, and Kitt continued, "Three of my girlfriends from college, and two from my former employer.  I haven't spent much time with any of them since I started my business.  I call them, but they are also busy so, I thought it would be good for all of us to get together today just to have some girlfriend time."

"Sounds great! It will be good to see the ladies."

Henri brought April a glass of champagne which she enjoyed while she and Kitt caught up with each other. They had not noticed that thirty minutes had passed when Henri returned with two menus asking if they would like to make their tea selections. Kitt looked at her watch. "Wow! Where are the other ladies? I didn't realize the time. Maybe I should call them." Kitt asked Henri to give them a few minutes before returning to take their tea selection.

April continued to sip her champagne while she watched Kitt's face drop with disappointment with each phone call that she made to her friends. When Kitt had made the last call, she could see the emotion welling up, but waited until Kitt was able to verbalize what was going on.

"I can't believe this. Two of them said they 'forgot' and the other three said they just couldn't make it. No explanation. No apology. No nothing. I feel like such a fool. I had this all set up to share with my so-called friends, and they didn't bother to show up or call to say they weren't coming."

Attempting to make light of the situation, April grabbed Kitt's hand and said, "It's okay, girl. We will enjoy all of this!"

"I noticed that they had not been calling me or taking my calls. It seemed that when I called them, they were always busy and said that they would call me back.  But, they never did.  So, that's why I thought it would be good to take some time to get us all together today.  I even sent them handwritten invitations.  I feel so foolish!"

"What do you think is really going on with them?" April asked.

"Well, I noticed they started treating me differently the last time we all got together.  I was feeling good about the business and told them how I landed the contract and had hired four employees.  At first, I thought that the side glances between them and changing the subject was my imagination because I just could not even begin to fathom that my friends would not share my excitement."

Henri returned with the tea menus.  Kitt told her that it would only be the two of them, and she would like to move to a table for two to free up the large table for other customers.  She felt foolish sitting at the table with all of the empty chairs when it was just her and April.

After Henri graciously moved them and brought their pots of tea and watercress sandwiches, April grabbed Kitt's hand once again.  "Not everyone in your circle will share your dream with you. Just like it was okay to have a dream, and it was okay to make it happen, it is now okay to be successful and to appreciate what you've achieved regardless of what others think.  You can't force them to celebrate your accomplishments; past, present or future.  It is what it is.  Keep it moving."

"I guess you are right." Henri had brought them both a second glass of champagne which Kitt raised and April followed suit. "To us. And, to my so-called friends, I say, 'Don't hate. Appreciate!' "

# Chapter 5

## PERMISSION TO "DO YOU"

*"Always be a first rate version of yourself instead of a second rate version of somebody else."*
- Judy Garland


"How've you been, girl," Kitt asked April sensing that something was a little off with her.  Even through the telephone, she could sense that her mood was a little down.

"I honestly don't want to go to my cousin's bridal shower today," April confided in Kitt.

"Really?  Why not?" Kitt asked surprised.

"I'm just so uncomfortable when I'm around my cousins.  They are all married with children and think that I should be married or at least dating someone."

Kitt totally understood where April was coming from.  "I know what you mean!  What is that about? Just because you reach a certain age, people think you should be married."

"Yes!  And my cousins even started setting me up with blind dates.  If I start telling you about some of the dates that I've been on that were total disasters, it would take us the rest of the day."  Kitt laughed with her friend, but understood how this was bothering her.

"Coming from another single woman, how do you feel about the whole dating, marriage and family thing?" Kitt asked.

"I don't know. I'm so into my career that I don't think about it much. I only think about it when I have to attend a corporate or social function, and I need a date."

"Yeah, me too." Kitt wanted to share more with her friend. "I really would like to be married with a family, but then I started my business and my life took a totally different path. I meet successful guys all the time, but they don't seem interested in me. One guy even told me that I intimidate men because of my success. Isn't that just crazy?"

April was glad she was having this conversation with Kitt. It was good that someone else understood and was not putting pressure on her to do or be something that she was not ready to do or be. "It does sound crazy, but there's probably some truth to it. Think about it. Look at the car you drive and the house you live in. You make your own money. Most men would wonder what they could do for you that you aren't already doing for yourself."

*Wow! Really? I never thought of it that way.* Surprised by her friend's perspective, Kitt asked, "Really? Do you seriously think men consider all of that? If that is the case, I may never find my mate. And the same is true for you. Look at how successful you are as a lawyer. You made partner in your firm early in your career. I want to be in a relationship, but it sounds like you don't."

"Not really," April once again confided. "Again, I don't even think about dating until I need an escort for a formal function. Like my cousin's upcoming wedding. I know that if I show up without a date, that will be the conversation the entire time, not to mention them trying to set me up with every single man there. Once they tried to set me up with a man thirty years older than me just because he was single. I think he must have had arthritis or something because he could barely move on the dance floor. That doesn't even make any sense."

Kitt burst into laughter, but April wasn't laughing. "That is too funny, April! Maybe he just couldn't dance. Don't assume that just because he's older, he has arthritis!"

"Who will they set me up with this time? Someone on oxygen?" April had to laugh at her own joke.

Kitt almost lost her breath laughing with her friend. When she recovered, she said, "Seriously, though, I can see how you would be uncomfortable going to your cousin's wedding."

"They think that I should be married by now based on my age. But, when I look at them, not all of them are happy. Don't get me wrong, some of them have great marriages and terrific kids, but maybe that's not for me," April shared her feelings with Kitt.

"I think other people hear our biological clocks ticking louder than we do. I know a few of my friends from college have good marriages, or at least they seem to. But, I also have friends that have already been divorced. When I think about that, I know that I would rather be single than be in a bad relationship," Kitt related.

"Right! Plus, what gives others the right to determine the proper time for me to get married? One of my cousins had the nerve to plan my wedding for me. She gave me a scrapbook for my birthday a couple of years ago that she had designed around plans for my wedding. I wasn't even dating anyone! Now, that takes a lot of nerve," April said.

"What?! That is crazy," Kitt laughed. "But, this can be one of those challenges on our life journey. I think you may have put your career first when your family thinks that you should have focused more on marriage and family. I know that they are proud of all that you've accomplished, yet when you think about it, there is never what we call the 'right time.' Suppose you had deferred your dream of being a partner in your law firm until after you found a husband?"

April valued Kitt's viewpoint. "I agree. I just wish my family could see it that way. Just because I'm a certain age doesn't mean that a relationship will just magically happen. If it does, it does, but I'm not stressing about it and I'm still going to focus on my career. If I meet 'Mr. Right' and we decide to get married and have children, then that will be the right time."

"Exactly," Kitt agreed with her friend. "Until then, just continue to 'do you.'"

# Chapter 6

## PERMISSION TO BE FIRST
*"Love yourself first and everything else falls into line."*
- Lucille Ball

Another busy week behind her, Kitt was looking forward to connecting with April.  She hung up her cell phone after trying to reach April for the fourth time.  She was beginning to get worried.  She and April usually talked every Saturday morning, sometimes making plans to meet for breakfast or hit the mall for a little shopping.  But, not today.  April loved talking on the phone, and it was unlike like her to not answer when she could, particularly on the weekends.  She always responded to voice mail messages.  Kitt didn't like leaving voice mail messages, but had left one for April after she didn't answer her first three phone calls.

*I just hope she is ok,* Kitt prayed silently.  *And I hope that I hear from her soon.*

Kitt was in the grocery store stocking up for the week ahead when her cell phone rang.  Her heart stopped beating when she saw a phone number on her caller id that she didn't recognize.  She cautiously pressed the answer button to receive the call, afraid of what she would hear on the other end.

"This is Kitt," she answered.

"Hey, girl." It was April. Kitt finally breathed a sigh of relief.

"April! Thank, God! Where are you? I've been calling you all day! Where are you calling from? I don't recognize this phone number."

"Girl, I'm in the hospital."

"What?! Which hospital? What happened?"

April, being the secret drama queen that she was, loved Kitt's excited, concerned response. "I'm at the Community Hospital. I had to come by ambulance. There was no time to call you."

"Oh my God!" Kitt exclaimed. "I'm on my way!" she said ditching the shopping cart she had filled with groceries, hanging up her cell phone and running out of the grocery store across the parking lot to her car. She had to get to her friend.

When Kitt reached the hospital room, she saw her best friend lying in bed connected to intravenous medications and all types of monitors. She ran to her, a little afraid to hug her, but hugging her anyway. "Hey, sweetie. What happened to you?"

Still reveling in the drama, April explained, "When I woke up this morning, the room was spinning, and I couldn't see out of my left eye."

"Why didn't you call me?"

"Duh! I couldn't see, and the room was spinning?" They both laughed at April's sarcasm.

"I'm sorry, girl," Kitt said still laughing. "Seriously, though. How are you feeling? What are the doctors saying?"

"They are still running tests, but they think it's due to an autoimmune disorder that I have."

Her heart sinking, April sat on the bed beside her friend, "I didn't know. I'm so sorry." She wondered why her friend had not shared this news with her before and wondered how long she had known. Or, if this was totally new. She wanted to know, but instead of prying, she decided to find out if she could do anything for April.

"Hey, do you need me to call your office on Monday to let them know that you won't be in?"

"No. That won't be necessary. I quit my job yesterday."

Not understanding, Kitt asked as gently as possible, "You quit your job? Why?"

"I was diagnosed with the disease a couple of months ago. At that time, my doctor warned me that stress could and probably would bring on episodes of sickness and symptoms. It turns out, she was correct. I tried to work through it, but I haven't felt that well in the past couple of weeks. I wasn't feeling well yesterday, but I went in to work anyway. For some reason, still unknown to me, the Senior Partner totally lost his mind with me. I don't know what happened to him, but he started screaming and yelling at me like I was his child. I've never seen him behave that way."

"How totally unprofessional," Kitt responded.

"Not only that, but just generally bad behavior for someone in authority," April agreed. "So, I got up and closed the door so that others in the office would not hear his tirade. I attempted to get to the root of whatever had set him off, but he just kept ranting and raving. I could feel my body responding, and I remembered what my doctor said about managing my stress level. When I couldn't reason with him, I decided that I had to put myself first. While he was still screaming at me, I started to pack my personal belongings."

"Wow," was all that Kitt managed to say.

Continuing with her story, "He was so caught up in whatever was bothering him, he didn't even notice me typing my letter of resignation. I printed it, handed it to him, gathered my belongings and walked out. I feel like I made the right decision."

Kitt pictured April walking out on her boss in his mid-sentence rant and wanted to high-five her. "You go, girl!" she said, reaching for her friend's hand. She gave her a loving squeeze to let her know that she supported her.

"But, what will you do now?" Kitt had to ask.

"Thankfully, I have enough savings to sustain me for a year. So, once I get out of here and get my health back on track, I will either find another law firm to join or I will go into private practice. The most important thing for me is to be able to work, but to also manage my stress level."

"I'm glad to hear that you plan to get back to work. You are such a good lawyer, and you have so much to offer," Kitt genuinely said to her friend.

"Oh, yeah! I want to keep working, but you know, in that moment when my boss was going off, and I started to not feel well, I knew that I had to put myself first. I know that most people would think that I was crazy for literally walking off of the job, but I feel like I made the decision that was best for me at the time. Would I suggest that someone else do the same thing as I did? The advice that I would give is to do what is in the individual's best interest."

"Not everyone can walk away like you did," Kitt concurred. "But, I totally agree that we need to make ourselves a priority and oftentimes, as women, we don't do that. I don't condone staying on a job if it is detrimental to our mental or physical health. For someone that can't walk away like you did, I would recommend that they develop a viable exit or transition strategy that would work for them."

Squeezing April's hand again, Kitt smiled at her and said, "I totally support your decision. You and your health should be your first priority."

"Now, how long before we can break you out of this joint?" Kitt asked, finally relieved that her friend would be alright.

# Chapter 7

## PERMISSION TO MAKE A MISTAKE
*"The real test is not whether you avoid this failure, because you won't. It's whether you let it harden or shame you into inaction, or whether you learn from it; whether you choose to persevere."*
— President Barack Obama

*How did this happen?* Kitt was wracking her brain trying to figure out exactly what she had done to cause her company to be in the "red" financially. She had gone over and over her bank statements, and while she could not see anything glaring, she had a sick feeling in her stomach. She made an appointment to meet with her accountant.

Her accountant, Linda, was quick with her response. "Business has been down since the economy crashed overall last year, but you still have the same number of employees on your payroll. You continue to pay the same amount of staff, but you no longer have the revenue to support that. It's just that simple."

As business increased, Kitt had added eleven marketing designers to the original staff of four. Within a short period of time, the economy suffered a significant downturn, which eventually resulted in a decrease of business for Kitt's company.

"Why didn't you say something?!" Kitt screamed at Linda. "You are supposed to be my accountant!" she blamed.

Linda was surprisingly calm with her response. "Kitt, we had this conversation at the end of the year last year. I asked you to consider down-sizing because of the economy and your response was, 'I'm sure it will get better. I don't want anyone losing their job.' I felt that you made that decision based on emotion instead of intelligence, but I didn't feel that it was my place to take it any further."

Kitt did remember the conversation which made her feel worse. It was all her fault. Now, not only was her company suffering, she would probably have to lay off some, if not most of her staff, the very thing she had attempted to avoid.

*God, please help me*, she prayed. She thanked Linda, picked up her purse and left the building. She drove straight to April's.

April could tell by the look on Kitt's face that she should open a bottle of red wine. That usually calmed them both down. After skillfully removing the cork and pouring them both a glass of Merlot, she looked directly at Kitt saying, "Okay. Tell me what's wrong."

"It's pretty bad, April. I have made a bad decision that might cost me my company, put my employees at risk and ultimately destroy my relationships with all of them." She recapped the conversation that she had just had with Linda.

April took a sip of her wine. *This is not good*, she thought, but didn't say it to Kitt. More than anything, Kitt needed her support right now. She reached across the bistro table and took Kitt's hand. "We have to touch and feel this problem before we can fix it. So, here is what I want you to do. I want you to go home, get in touch with how you are feeling; get in bed and cry all night if you need to. Then, when you are done with your emotions, call me, and we will come up with a transition plan that will work for everyone. Including you."

Kitt broke down. Reality had set in. The tears started flowing, and she could not speak. April let her have her moment. When Kitt was finally able to speak, she said, "How could I let this happen? I feel like such a failure. I'm sure that my so-called friends will have a ball talking about me once the news gets out. And here I am, the big CEO, crying my eyes out like a baby. This is so weak."

"Listen to me. You cannot control what others say. They are going to talk whether they have the correct information or not. That is just human nature. You have to decide how you are going to respond to it."

"As for crying - what? You think that because you have a big title that you stop being a woman? Do you think that you stop having feelings? Where is the rule written that because you own a business that you can't cry, or laugh for that matter? You didn't stop being human when you started your business."

"I know that you are right, but I can't help feeling like such a total failure."

"Do you think that you are the only one who ever lost a business?  Look at Donald Trump.  He lost and sprang back multiple times."

"I know.  I know that you are right, but how can I ever be in business again after this?"  Kitt responded through her tears.

"You only fail if you don't learn from it.  This is an opportunity to grow, to do better and to be a better business owner.  Learn from this 'mistake' for lack of a better word.  'Failures' are opportunities for us to learn if we take advantage of the lesson.  I know that you can't see that right now, but you will.  Once you get on the other side of all of this, you will be much better for it."

April silently prayed that her words were helpful.  And that Kitt would indeed have another chance in business.  But, mostly that she would get through this.

# Chapter 8

## PERMISSION TO LET GO

*"To be yourself in a world that is constantly trying to make you something else is the greatest accomplishment."*
- Ralph Waldo Emerson


It was indeed a tough time emotionally, but Kitt managed to shut down her company without too much harm to her employees or to her customers. She was able to transition her customers to another firm similar to her company and most of her employees were even employed by the firm as well. It was an informal corporate acquisition, but it worked for everyone.  Although, the pieces seem to fall into place, it was still a difficult time for Kitt.  It was a major loss to her since she had devoted so much of herself to building her company.

After the company changeover was complete, The most grim part for Kitt was that she had to make the decision to get back into the mainstream by becoming someone else's employee again.  The company that took over her contracts and employees had offered her a Vice-President position.  Kitt knew that she was not in a financial position to turn it down.  April agreed with her and convinced her to accept the offer.

While it provided a steady income stream, it was not the income or freedom to which Kitt had become accustomed since starting her company. In the midst of another melt down, April, yet again, had to talk her friend down.

"So what, that you have to turn in your Mercedes and drive a Toyota? It's a reliable car, and the dealer has given you a deal that will work for your current income," April advised her friend. They were sitting in the Mercedes dealership waiting for the Sales Consultant to return with paperwork for Kitt to end the lease on her Mercedes. April had assisted in the negotiation for an early lease termination without a hefty penalty. Kitt appreciated her for it and knew that she could never afford to pay her friend for all of the free legal assistance that she so willing gave to her.

"That's easy for you to say since you are still styling around town in your phat Benz," Kitt said solemnly. She was sorry as soon as she said it. She knew what a gift of time and intelligence her friend was giving her, and she didn't want to offend her. She was also concerned about April's health, but had been so focused on herself lately, that she had forgotten to ask April how she was feeling.

She quickly adjusted her attitude. "I know. I'm sorry, girl. Thanks for helping me with this. Hey- how have you been feeling?" she asked, genuinely concerned.

"I'm feeling great since I quit my job and that last hospital visit. And, I do know what you are going through. I decided that I'm definitely not going to go back to work for at least a year. I want to focus on my health, so I've modified my lifestyle to support my decision."

"Really?" Kitt asked, intrigued.

"Yep. I still 'style around town' in my Benz, as you say, but I have downsized quite a bit. I've sold a lot of clothing, jewelry, expensive handbags, appliances and stuff that I don't need for some extra cash. I'm also watching my spending. I'm thinking of selling my townhome for a smaller condo."

"Wow!" Kitt said surprised to hear that her friend was also going through a similar transition. "I had no idea."

"I know. You've been going through a lot lately, so I didn't say anything. I'm only still driving my Benz because it's paid for. I thought about selling it and getting a lower maintenance vehicle, but that will come later. Right now, I'm focused on not living beyond my means and letting go of the material things that I enjoyed at one time, but no longer have a purpose in my life."

"I can't believe you are selling your Louis and Guccis! You LOVE those purses. I bet you had a good twenty to thirty-thousand dollars worth of leather!"

"You are probably right. Those were just the ones that you saw." They both laughed. April continued, "You know, it was a very different time in my life.  Buying expensive clothes, shoes, purses and jewelry was how I rewarded myself for hard work, and I had the income to support it.  But, now I'm in a much different place, and those things don't have the same value for me.  The quality of my life is the most important."

Kitt sighed.  "I hear you.  I'm just not there, yet. I know that I need to make some changes as well since my income is nowhere near what it used to be. There is just so much going on with me.  You made the decision to quit your job.  For me, I NEVER thought that I would have to go back to work for someone else.  And the worst part is that I have to report to 'Barbie.' "

"Your new boss' name is Barbie?" April asked, somewhat confused.

"No, her name is Denise, but I call her Barbie because she is not much older than twelve years old, and I feel like her mother."

April laughed aloud at Kitt's analogy of her new boss and was glad that she still had her sense of humor through it all.  "Girl, that is too funny!  You are not even forty yet, so how young can she be?"

"Younger than me, and not as experienced.  I think that is the toughest part for me.  After building a million dollar business, now I have to go back to work and answer to someone again.  Along with that, I need to do the same thing that you are doing: downsizing.  Turning in this car is just the first step. I'm sure that I'm going to need to change my lifestyle, too. I guess I can say 'goodbye' to shopping whenever I feel like it, going out to dinner and stuff, huh? It doesn't matter much anyway since I cannot even buy a friend right now. You are the only one who always hangs in there with me through thick and thin." Kitt decided to be totally honest with her friend. "I can't quiet the dialogue from my ego:

> *'You are not the CEO anymore!'*
> *'What is everyone saying?'*
> *'You are driving a Toyota now!'*
> *'You have to report to Barbie!'*
> *'You have to be at work at a certain time every day again!'*
> *'No more champagne dinners!'*
> *'You know that you are going to have to sell that house!' "*

April thought of how proud Kitt was when she'd moved into her new home not too long ago. She hated all of this for her friend, but she honestly knew that Kitt would need to make some changes and sacrifices to get back on track. The people that Kitt used to wine and dine and hang out with were only along for the ride. Now that the ride is over, they are long gone. They were never her friends. It sucks, but that's life.

"I hear you, girl. But, you know, it's only temporary. It's just something that you need to do in order to get to the next phase of your life. You cannot move forward as long as you are holding on to the past.  Who knows why things happen the way that they do?  I do know that you cannot have something new as long as you have a tight grip on the old stuff.  I believe that everything will work out for you.  God is on your side, and you have everything you need to make it through and to be better on the other side of this."

To make a final point, April added, "As far as making the changes in your life, toxic relationships and the material things - it's called letting go."

# Chapter 9

## PERMISSION TO "RE-DO" YOU
*"Nothing can dim the light which shines from within."*
-Maya Angelou


Time seemed to fly for both Kitt and April. Life continued to present ups and downs, obstacles and triumphs. No matter what challenges beset them, their friendship remained true and strong. It seemed as though, over time, they could read each other's thoughts.

*Where has the time gone and what has happened to my body?* Kitt thought as she sat across from April at their favorite countryside restaurant. She wanted to eat another dinner roll, but thought about the rolls forming around her midsection and decided against it.

"Girl, have another roll. It's not going to hurt you. You only live once." April saw Kitt glance at the bread basket, then quickly look away.

*How does she do that?!* "Nope. I'm going to pass. My hips are spreading across the entire tri-state area. How did this happen?"

"Listen to you, Ms. 'size two'. You have been the same size ever since we met so many years ago. Gosh! Where has the time gone?"

"That's exactly what I was just thinking! How come no one prepared us for middle age?" Kitt asked despairingly.

"You know what Oprah used to say. 'Fifty is the new thirty!' " April said with a laugh.

"That's bull! Fifty is fifty. We are not there yet, but it won't be much longer. When I was a kid, I remember thinking that fifty was so old. And now, here I am, knocking on Fifty's door! I am SO not ready!"

April laughed at her friend, but she knew there was some truth to what she was saying. "But, you have to say that being here and complaining about getting older, even though your body may not look the way you want, is so much better than the alternative."

Thoughtfully, Kitt responded, "Yeah. We have so much to be grateful for." She thought of April's health challenges over the years. She had made the right decision to quit her job years ago. Managing her stress level had probably made a huge difference in her quality of life. She had done well creating her law practice and able to be selective with her clients and their cases. Her health had been up and down, but overall, she was doing a great job managing it.

"I also noticed that our priorities have changed with time and maturity. You had that conversation with me when I had to close my company and give up some things in my life that I had become accustomed to. I have to admit that those things were just that:

things.  I'm not saying that I don't still enjoy material things, but I have a different appreciation now.  I won't waste my money on frivolous things, but I still enjoy a good bargain.  And this, us having dinner together, is an example of enjoying things differently.  We have always enjoyed a good meal together, but I feel that it's more about the fellowship now, don't you think?" Kitt asked, eagerly interested in April's answer.

"Absolutely!  I think we appreciate the gift of time and friendship more now that we have some years and life experience behind us," April answered, not anticipating Kitt's next question.

"If you had to do it all again, what you want to do in life?"

"Girl, you sound like we are ninety-nine years old and getting ready for Glory!  Don't be so morbid!"

"No! No, I'm not being morbid.  I've just been thinking a lot lately about the quality of life and reflecting on the years and just wondering how things could have been different had I made different choices."

Thinking that she knew where Kitt was going with this conversation, she asked, "Is this about having to go back to work after you closed your company?  Everything turned out pretty good for you.  I think you are doing well as an independent contractor.  You have the best of both worlds.  You don't have a company to run, and you have the flexibility and income that you want."

Kitt had decided to leave the Vice-President position and go out on her own again, but this time as an independent contractor without employees. She was more comfortable with this structure since it required that she was only responsible for herself.

"Yeah, but as I get older, I have to now deal with Barbie AND Ken in leadership positions," Kitt said jokingly. April remembered Kitt making a similar statement about having to report to younger people in executive positions when she went back to work after closing her company.

Kitt continued, "I've forgotten more stuff than they know about their own jobs. It's tough, but, hey, I know that I have to make a living."

Kitt's statement made April laugh, but she knew there was an important underlying reason for this conversation that had been started.

"I'm not sure what I would have done differently. I've always wanted to be a lawyer. I can't think of doing anything else and I'm satisfied with my career. What about you? What's your calling?"

Hesitantly, Kitt responded, "I don't know…"

"Awwww… come on now! I know there is something that you want to share. Come on, girl. Do tell!" April plied, impatiently wanting an answer.

Cautiously, Kitt did share, "Well… I've always wanted to be a writer. I've been secretly working on a novel for a few years." *I hope she doesn't think that I'm crazy.* Kitt braced herself for April's response.

"Really?" April said, surprised. "So, what are you writing about?"

"It's just a fictional story about relationships that we have in life. I guess you could call it 'fiction with a message.' " *I can't believe that I just came out of the closet as a writer. Hopefully, April won't ask me anything else. I'm sorry that I brought it up!*

"Can I read it?" April asked, sincerely interested in Kitt's work.

*Oh, NO!* "I don't know. You might not be interested, and it might not be any good."

"Do you think it's good?"

"Hell yeah, I think it's good," Kitt answered too quickly and defensively.

"So, you do think it's good! And that tells me that you really like writing! Why haven't you pursued writing before?"

"No one will take me seriously as a novelist. People know me and see me as a marketing professional. Who would buy my books?"

"Hmmm...sounds like the same questions you had before you started your business. Once you quieted all of that internal negative noise swirling around in your head, look at what happened. You went on to build a successful business and also helped a lot of people who needed jobs."

"Yeah, and I don't even have the same passion for marketing that I have for writing," April shared before she realized what she was saying.

"Aha! There it is! That magic word that makes the difference between doing something that we are good at to generate a paycheck versus doing what we really love. Passion. It sounds like you definitely have a passion for writing."

"I really do," Kitt decided to be honest. "When I write, I get lost in my own story. And it's so much fun creating the characters and their stories. I just don't know how to go from a marketing consultant to fiction writer."

"It doesn't have to happen overnight. And who says that you can't be both? You can write in the evenings after work and on the weekends. It sounds like it wouldn't even interfere with your work," April said matter-of-factly. She added, "People recreate themselves all of the time. Our parents chose a job or a career and stayed with it for thirty years until they retired. That was the way of their world. The world we live in is much different now. Haven't you heard the new buzz words: 'Re-career'; 'Re-invent'; 'Re-do you?' "

" 'Re-do you'? That is too funny!" Kitt laughed. "But, I kinda like it!"

"Yeah? Maybe you should try it!"

*I think I will*, Kitt thought. *I am going to finally be true to myself.*

# Chapter 10

## PERMISSION TO BE HONEST

*"One of the lessons that I grew up with was to always stay true to yourself and never let what somebody else says distract you from your goals."*
- Michelle Obama

Kitt had no idea how much joy writing brought to her until she made the time and commitment to finish her novel. She still had some fear and trepidation to share her work with others, but she gave into her passion and continued to write despite the internal rockets of doubt firing off in her head.

*Am I wasting my time?*
*Will anyone like my book?*
*Will they change their perception of me because of my writing?*
*Will anyone buy my book?*
*Will anyone take me seriously as an author?*
*I can't compete with the popular authors.*
*Did I wait too long to try to become a writer?*

There were intervals when Kitt allowed her internal dialogue of doubt to take over, and she would not write. It was those times that the blue funk also crept in. It didn't take her long to realize that when she was writing, she was happy. One day it finally dawned on her. *I guess this is what passion feels like.* And she had to smile.

She called April when the manuscript was finished. She was a little nervous when she announced to her best friend, "Well...it's finished. I finished my book!"

"Awesome! When can I read it?" April was excited.

"Read it? Really? You want to read it?" Kitt asked surprised.

"Yes, I want to read it!"

"Okay. But, you have to promise to give me honest feedback!" Kitt begged.

"Always. Now, e-mail it to me, password protected."

Kitt made a copy of the manuscript, password protected it and e-mailed it to April. She had to admit to herself that she was still afraid, but mostly excited.

*I should have finished the book sooner. I let fear and doubt get in my way. I let myself get in my own way. I honestly ENJOY writing more than anything. I know that most authors don't make a lot of money from selling books, but who knows what may come of it?*

It was four in the morning when Kitt heard her phone ring. She saw on her caller id that it was April. Worried, she answered right away. "April? What's wrong? Are you okay?"

"No.  I'm not okay.  I've been up all night reading this fantastic novel that you wrote and wondering why you kept your writing talent a secret all of this time!"

Exhaling relief, Kitt smiled, "You scared me to death!  I thought you were sick calling me this time of morning!"  She was interested in what April thought of her book.  "So, you liked it?  You are not just saying that because you are my friend?"

"Heck no!  You know that I would tell you the truth.  And you know that I wouldn't be up this early just to talk.  You are a good writer!  So, what are you going to do with this book?"

*I'm over forty.  I don't like my day job anymore. It's time to be honest with myself and true to my passion.*

Knowing that actually saying the words would begin to bring her dream to reality, Kitt answered, "I'm going to publish it."

"Yippee!  Now you are talking!"

"I am still going to continue to work my marketing gigs, because we both know that I can't afford to not work.  But, I'm going to pursue self-publishing the novel; and I think that I will also write a blog or maybe some other content for business owners.  There is a lot of information about how to succeed in business, but not enough on how to handle, and possibly avoid the pitfalls and challenges in business.  I am going to interview other business owners to develop content that will be helpful to others who may have had a situation similar to mine. I surely could have used something like that years ago. And maybe even now as I embark on this new adventure," she said feeling relieved.

"This is exciting. I'm glad to hear that. You sound more self-assured than I can ever remember."

"I decided that it's time to finally be honest with myself and not focus so much on 'them' and what 'they' say. Maybe, it's middle age," Kitt said. "I always thought that we should work to get rich or to have a certain lifestyle or to have an important title. But, recently I realized that there must be more to this thing we call 'life.' I honestly enjoy writing more than I ever enjoyed marketing. It doesn't feel like work. I look forward to it; I enjoy it, I'm good at it, so, I'm going to do it."

To seal the deal for herself, Kitt added, "And since time is moving, and we aren't getting any younger, if I don't do it now, then when?"

# Chapter 11

## PERMISSION TO SERVE
*"For unto whom much is given, much is required."*
- The Holy Bible

Kitt was in love with her new profession. She self-published her novel and started a weekly blog and online radio show for others also in transition and wanting to follow their passion. The novel was doing well, and the blog and radio show took off with popularity. She was often asked to speak to professional organizations for which she was paid, but also spoke to non-profit organizations and provided mentorship to young entrepreneurs for free. Kitt found the combination of work and volunteerism the perfect balance for her life. She was meeting a lot of great people doing spectacular things in business and their personal lives.

As always, she shared this newfound joy with her best friend as they enjoyed a glass of sparkling water at their favorite harbor restaurant. "I am in such a good place right now. It's unbelievable. I never knew the value of volunteerism until I started mentoring young entrepreneurs. You know, they could benefit from someone like you, with your legal background."

April took a sip of her water, set her glass on the table and looked at Kitt with eyes rolled to the top. "I know that you don't think that I'm going to give away legal service for free. You must have lost your mind. I enjoy my free time, and I'm not willing to share it with anyone. Call me 'selfish.' "

" 'Selfish!' " They laughed together. "Seriously- you can't tell me that you don't have one hour per week to volunteer to help others. Tell me why not."

April was quick with her response, "You tell me why I should!"

"I'll tell you why I do it. I do it because I feel incredibly blessed. When I look back on my journey and all that God has brought me through, I know that I have to share my skill and my knowledge to help others on their journey. I didn't plan it this way, but I know this was God's plan for me. I had to go through all of my own stuff in order to have something meaningful to share. It's hard to explain. I get a sense of enjoyment, and helping others is also helping me to continue to grow somehow."

April was holding strong to her position. "It might work for you, but I don't see it working for me. I have no interest in giving away an hour of my time."

Kitt was not willing to give up just yet. "Okay, then do me a favor. Come with me to the Small Business Center tomorrow morning for one hour. There will be some new business owners there that will need some legal guidance; simple stuff like how to set up their business. Just help them, and I won't ask you anymore."

"Okay.  Whatever.  What time are you picking me up?"

"Thanks, girl!  I'll pick you up at nine o'clock sharp!" April said smiling.  *She is going to love it!*

Kitt and April walked into the Small Business Center at nine-thirty in the morning, greeted by the Director.  Kitt introduced April, cutting her eyes at her to indicate that she better be on her best behavior.  The Director was thrilled to meet April, put her arms around her and escorted her into a conference room where twenty people were seated, theatre style.  The Director brought April to the front of the room, excitedly announcing, "Good Morning everyone.  Our speaker for the morning has arrived.  Let's give her a warm welcome."  April cut her eyes at Kitt.  Kitt returned the glare with an assured smile.  She regretted having set up her friend like this, but she knew that she would be a big hit.

After applause from the eager group, the Director continued, "I know that you are all anxious to hear what our speaker has to say about the various business organizational structures available.  So, I'm going to get out of her way and let her begin."

Kitt stood in the back of the room, where she thought it was safe.  Even from where she stood, she noticed that it only took a few seconds for April to absorb why she was there, and the information needed by her audience.  Kitt already knew that this was a topic that April could speak on in her sleep.

And so, she began.  Kitt exhaled, knowing that she had made the right decision bringing April in.  She watched her friend transform and share her expert knowledge as the group hung onto her every word.

April became animated as she imparted information, and more engaged with each question from the audience.  After one hour, the Director returned to the front of the room and stood next to April.  "Wow," she said.  "We are getting some good information, but our time is up.  Let's give a round of applause to our speaker for sharing her time and a wealth of knowledge with us today."  Everyone applauded, and one hand went up from a young man sitting on the front row.

After he was acknowledged by the Director, he directed his question to April, "Is there any way that we could get in contact with you?  I could really use your help."

Kitt held her breath, hoping that the session wouldn't go south at this point.  April turned to the whiteboard, picked up a black marker and wrote her name and office phone number.  "You can reach me on this number.  But, I'll be glad to come back again next week.  If that's possible?" she asked turning to the Director for an answer.

"Absolutely!" she exclaimed, not hiding her excitement.  "We've been in need of someone like you for a long time, but we could not find anyone willing to volunteer their time," she said exchanging a knowing look with Kitt.

Kitt patiently waited in the back of the room, watching each attendee as they approached April to individually express their appreciation for the information that she had presented. April delighted in the attention that she received. Kitt could not be more pleased with the outcome.

After everyone had left the room, April made her way from the front to the back where Kitt was still standing, partially afraid to move or to speak, not sure what April would say to her.

"Let's go have an early lunch," April said.

Somewhat surprised, Kitt answered, "Okay. Sure. Your choice of restaurant." Not wanting to wait, she asked, "So, are you really coming back next week?"

April quickly turned with a surprised look and pointedly said, "Yes, I'm coming back next week! These people need me!"

Kitt smiled, speaking within, *"Mission accomplished."*

# Chapter 12

## PERMISSION TO TRUST

*"As long as you are still in the game, you have a chance to win!"*
- Kathleen Driver

"How long have we been friends?" Kitt asked April. They were sitting together enjoying tea at the Ritz-Carlton. Although management had changed a few times over the years, Kitt and April remained loyal, frequent customers.

"I don't know. Thirty years, maybe?" They had both celebrated the big 5-0 this year by taking a two-week Caribbean cruise.

"Wow. Where has the time gone? It's hard to believe that we are both fifty! And we are still friends!" Kitt said.

"Yep. I should have kicked your butt to the curb years ago," April joked with her friend.

Kitt laughed with April, but replied seriously, "I'm so glad that you didn't. In case I never told you, I know that you are a true, devoted friend. I don't know what I would have done without you. Especially during my many bumps in the road."

"You've been a great friend to me as well," said April, sipping her tea.

"As a child, did you ever think about what your life would look like at fifty?" Kitt inquired, eager to hear what April had to say.

"No, I didn't.  I just remember thinking that fifty was really old!" she said laughing.

"I know!  Me too!  But, I don't feel old at all. I'm not ready to just sit around and knit or watch television all day.  I feel like I still have a lot to offer. I'm not even ready to retire, yet."

"That's because you are still making a valuable contribution through your work and your volunteerism.  Your writing is still going well and I can see how passionate you are helping out at the Small Business Center."  Kitt and April both now volunteered there at least one day a week, often riding together.  April became fully engaged after that very first day when she presented to the group of twenty eager and receptive young entrepreneurs just a few years ago.

Kitt always held heartfelt appreciation for April.  She always gave her the truth, no matter how much it would hurt.  "Thanks for saying that.  I really do enjoy writing and helping out however I can at the Small Business Center.  Do you remember how scared I was to actually pursue writing?"

"I do remember," April said, inwardly reflecting on the conversation she and Kitt had back then. "What do you think was the most pivotal in moving you forward with your writing?"

"I think it was being honest with myself about what I really wanted to do.  As you said back then, it was about following my passion."  Giving critical thought back to that time, Kitt resumed, "I also think that trust was a huge factor."

Interested in where Kitt was going with her thoughts, April asked, "Trust?  Really?  How so?"

"Once I gave myself permission to follow my passion for writing, I had to trust that God had planted that desire within me and also blessed me with the talent and creativity to actually be a good writer.  I had to trust that God would put everything and everyone in the right place at the right time in order for me to be successful."

After a few moments of comfortable silence between them, Kitt continued, "I think that we owe our best to God for blessing us with the gift of life.  We also owe it to ourselves to get the most out of life and to give the most while we can.  We only pass this way once, and we should make the best of it.  God gives us everything that we need, we just need to stay connected and be open, willing and ready to receive all that He has for us."

April contemplated what her friend had just shared with her.  Focusing on what Kitt said about being honest with herself, she responded, "I understand what you are saying.  Once you let go of the fear and the conversations going on in your head about 'what will THEY think?' And 'what will THEY say?' it seems as though you had peace and acceptance. When I say 'acceptance,' I mean self-acceptance."

Kitt agreed, "Right you are, my friend. It's just human nature to consider what others will think of us, but at the end of the day, we have to live with our decisions. Once I realized that I really wanted to write, I had to let go of the fear and once again step out on faith."

"I'm glad that you answered your internal call to follow your dream. Not once, but twice. Remember, your business started with a dream; then your novel and your blog." Switching the subject before Kitt had a chance to interrupt her, April opinioned, "It's such a shame that society has placed a stigma on age fifty in the workplace. I know so many people who have been downsized due to age, or retired, but cannot continue to work or return to work because of their age."

"It is a shame, because life is not over just because we reached fifty. Look at us. We have so much left to offer. I'm glad that you still have your law practice, and I'm comfortable with marketing consulting, writing and volunteering at the Small Business Center. I think that starting a business is a great retirement plan. I wish that more people our age would think about how they can successfully and financially incorporate a small business into their retirement planning. That can be one way of proactively planning just in case they are the victim of age discrimination in corporate America."

"Great thoughts!  Why don't we develop a workshop around that topic and offer it at the Small Business Center?  Our target audience can be the fifty-plus crowd," April proposed.

"I'm in!" Kitt said without hesitation.  They high-fived each other to seal the deal.

Back peddling just a bit, April asked "Do you think that we would have an audience?  Don't you think that baby boomers would shy away from starting a business?"

"Here is what I think.  Starting a business is a risk at any age.  I recently read that businesses started by baby boomers are more successful than businesses started by their grandkids.  This is due in part to the experience of the older generation.  Plus, I would add that if you have the desire to start a business, as long as it is not a financial risk, go for it.  You are still going to be fifty whether you start a business or not.  You won't get any younger by NOT starting the business, so why should being fifty stop you if it is something that you really want to do, and it won't be detrimental personally or financially?"

April laughed at Kitt's analogy.  She understood what she was trying to say.  But, also sensing that familiar creative spark from Kitt, April knew there was more going on that she was not yet sharing.  "So what's next for you as you begin the second phase of your life?  I can see your wheels spinning and I see that familiar fire in your eyes," she said warmly.

Kitt smiled. *She knows me so well.* "I don't know. I am in a comfortable place. I'm enjoying the balance of work, volunteering and free time. But, I have been thinking of some other things that I might want to do," she answered adding a sense of intrigue.

"I won't press you. Whatever it is, I'm glad I'm around to see you in action. And, I'm sure that you will be successful. I can't wait to see what happens next! Being your friend is definitely not boring."

"I've come to a place in my life where I realize that stuff will happen, but it's how we respond to it that really makes the difference. I learned a lot about that from you and I thank you for it."

Lifting her glass of champagne, Kitt toasted her long-time friend and confidante, "And as long as we are still here, in this experience of life, we have a chance to win!"

*Kathleen Driver resides in Prince George's County, Maryland. In addition to writing, she provides business coaching and consulting services. For more information, visit: www.mindyourbusinessllc.com.*

*For works of fiction, Ms. Driver writes under the penname of Elle Nora. For more information: www.readellenora.com. For a copy of her latest novel, Better Choices, visit www.amazon.com or link directly: http://www.amazon.com/dp/B00FHEQVM0.*

*Book Cover design by: Dream Designs*
*www.dreamdesignsgraphics.com*

www.ingramcontent.com/pod-product-compliance
Lightning Source LLC
Chambersburg PA
CBHW060647210326
41520CB00010B/1779